Ciara Platt is a young woman from North Idaho. Ever since she was a child, she's found solace in writing and sharing her thoughts. In 2022, she was hospitalized for schizoaffective disorder, bipolar type. She has since decided to share her journey with others in hopes that it would help normalize mental health and help others feel less alone. She is happily married with two small babies and finds great comfort in being a mom. She hopes to continue to use her voice as a tool to help end the stigma surrounding on mental health and encourages those around her to do the same.

Dedicated to all of those who are riding the waves of uncertainty, trying to grasp reality, and hoping for a future free of concern.

You are not alone in your thoughts. I'm here, C. Platt.

Angelo and my two sweet babies, Marley and Milo. You give me the strength to carry on and fight. Also, my parents and family for continuing to stand by my side and help me navigate the up and downs of my illness.

Ciara Platt

MIND OF A MIXED STATE

AUSTIN MACAULEY PUBLISHERS®

LONDON * CAMBRIDGE * NEW YORK * SHARJAH

Ordering Information
Quantity sales: Special discounts are available on quantity purchases by corporations, associations, and others. For details, contact the publisher at the address below.

Publisher's Cataloging-in-Publication data
Platt, Ciara
Mind of a Mixed State

ISBN 9798886936834 (Paperback)
ISBN 9798886936841 (ePub e-book)

Library of Congress Control Number: 2024901865

www.austinmacauley.com/us

First Published 2024
Austin Macauley Publishers LLC
40 Wall Street, 33rd Floor, Suite 3302
New York, NY 10005
USA

mail-usa@austinmacauley.com
+1 (646) 5125767

Thank you to Austin Macauley Publishing for making this book possible and encouraging me to use my voice on a larger platform.

Prologue

Everything written in this book was done while in the midst of a manic episode with psychotic features. My formal diagnosis is schizoaffective disorder, bipolar type as well as ADHD.

I can't define this book as fiction or non-fiction. It's merely my thoughts and a form of processing.

Please take what you will from it and leave what doesn't resonate.

I am only human.

Who Am I

You would think from the outside that I have it all together. The way my hair falls softly, my clothes yell, "pick me,", and my eyes twinkle with kindness.

That couldn't be further from the truth.

See, I want the illusion of control. I want everyone to feel safe in my presence and feel as though there isn't a care in the world to cling to. Who doesn't want the be free from concern in a world riddled with struggle?

I was around five years old when I started realizing that I was different. I would try bonding with kids my age and struggled. I felt like I could read people's mind based on their eyes. I would often see things that others say wasn't there. Oh, and to top it all off, I had severe trust issues. I never fully trusted surface level answers. I knew deep down, there was always more to the story… and I wanted to know what that more was. I wanted to know it all.

When I was seven, we moved to the states. No big deal; it was fun. I remember it as being abrupt. I remember feeling disconnected and sort of lost. The world I grew up in was now being rooted to an entirely new world. The people that I grew up knowing we're going to change and have new names with new faces. Everything I thought I knew was going to be shaken up and changed a bit. With change, comes bigger questions. I like to think I know the answers to those questions now that it's nearly twenty 20 years later. Maybe this book will help me understand those questions, maybe it will help me find the answers I so long for… Or maybe not.

Time Warp

How to make time go by when you're stuck in a psych unit…

1. If you're anything like me, you got in here kicking, screaming, and fighting the whole way down. "'Coming to'" has made this quite the challenge because my privileges. Aare essentially non-existent. I think I took close to 25 showers in the span of five days. I am clinging to whatever I can to *make the voices stop*. Shower. Dry off. Brush teeth. Repeat. Also, if you're anything like me, – you get to shower without a shower curtain because, apparently, it's a weapon for suicide. (Like REALLY, Ciara? A shower curtain??) Ugh, what was I even thinking?

2. Next, exercise. At first, this was tough because I think the nurses thought I was trying to escape anytime I jogged laps. What else is there when energy levels are high, and you're stuck in a mental hospital?

3. I prayed. Yep, goddammit, I did. I always told myself I wouldn't stoop to that level. Eh, I've been desperate enough. Sometimes I even pray just to

feel like I have a buddy to talk to. Being manic is wild that way. I fluctuate between really high energy and then intense delusions. At one point, I found myself praying repeatedly toward the demons off and feel like I had a friend by my side while doing so.

4. Wash your hands when allowed. This may sound like a funny one, but I also found a lot of solace in repeatedly scrubbing my hands.

5. When I was spotted doing more exercise, I was granted a yoga mat. USE THIS. I am terrible at yoga, but my body isn't designed to last forever and it's aching more and more the older I get. Stretch.

6. When I was finally granted phone privileges, I think after a week or so, I utilized this time to call family. This is a tricky one for some people because your family may not necessarily want to talk to you… and that's okay. Being mentally ill comes with its struggles and we have to respect the space some people need. Lucky for me, that wasn't the case this time around. When I got phone time, I took it. Hearing my kid's' voices is the best.

7. Getting a journal has been my favorite so far. I have so many thoughts, so many ideas, and it feels too challenging to keep them inside of me. I feel like I have a swarm of bees inside my body and if I don't set them free, they just eat me alive.

8. As a breastfeeding mom, I have the lovely pleasure of breastfeeding. When I feel the need to pump, I get excited because it kills a solid ten minutes or so.

It's like traveling to the future every moment. Got to do what keeps our mind busy and healthy.

9. One of my other favorite ways to kill the time, once my privileges got to this point, is connecting with others. Being on the main unit and out of the isolation room gives me more hope. I feel like connecting with others is all what we crave deep down. Our joy is only present when we have others to share it with.

People who help keep me grounded and inspire me: Gandhi, MLK Jr., my babies, my doctors, the nurses Everyone?

Faced With Reality

Sometimes, I think I'm on the brink of reality or that I'm disassociating from my true self. I get so caught up in the cloud of thinking, it can be a tad overbearing at times.

Having conversations with people is hard today. The cool thing about being around neurodiverse people though is that we all relate one way or another – which definitely helps pull me out of my own head.

I thought I was pretty crazy for putting patterns together and being extremely introspective… but you know what? I've learned that's super common with bipolar/schizoaffective. Medication seems to help me out by tugging on my shoulder and repeatedly saying, "Sshhhhh," and, "quiet down."

Fun thing about bipolar mania is that I feel I can be on top of the world, yet only about specific things, like; folding towels or walking the block 15 times. I like running, sometimes the bees in my body just need to swarm around and escape the hive. Running seems to help with that. It tones it down a bit.

Lastly, when fully privileged… ATTEND GROUPS. Do the art you feel, whatever it may be, and get it OUT.

Having it locked inside just makes it fester – me personally that is.

Growing Pains

Growing up is weird as fuck. I spent my whole childhood thinking that adults had the answers. Now that I am an adult, it feels the complete opposite. What is even going on? How am I supposed to navigate the shit-storm of adulthood while still healing the traumatized inner-child within me?

I just read some of my writing to another patient;, he told me it was really good but would probably get "Boo'd" a lot.

I don't know what I'm doing anymore. Being 26 is exhausting and I still have much more to do and go through. Wow, what a wild ride so far.

Robot Takeover

I'm not gonna stand a chance when the robots takeover because I fought six security guards in intensive inpatient and I did not end up winning that fight. If anything, I think I may have broken a couple of my wrist bones… I also think we don't stand a chance to the robot takeover because we built these damn machines and there are A LOT of smart humans. I know at least twenty20.

The biggest stress I'm facing currently is the mixed mania. I feel so exhausted mentally but I'm also on edge and a bit racy and agitated. It feels as though my thoughts are all scrambled up like eggs, but my body is firing neurons left and right like a damn Ping-Pong machine.

Maybe I relate to Forest Gump more than I think. He runs and runs and that's what I spend most of my time doing – running against the wind and rain. Staying strong but running wild.

The Feds Are Watching

What good reason would the feds have to watch me? I've never done anything wrong. Although I've been involved in a lot of politics, I haven't engaged in anything that should be on the wrong side of history. I'm proud of who I am and what I do. My brain just likes to trick me and make crazy things up. Luckily, my meds are helping me by saying, "calm down."

I'm excited to call Angelo and hear how he slept. I hope the phone isn't bugged still. I want to see him, and I hope I get too soon. I miss him so much and can't wait to cuddle him and watch some movies together. This whole experience has made me want to watch five movies:

* Eternal Sunshine of the Spotless Mind
* Silver Linings Playbook
* It's kind of a Funny Story
* Human Experience
* Mrs. Doubtfire

Additionally, my anxiety seems to be much higher in the morning versus the afternoon. Usually when I'm close to pumping, my anxiety sky-rockets and my paranoia sets back in. Hormones must be playing a huge role considering

I had two babies within two years. My system is truly out of whack between that and breastfeeding.

Did you know there's billions of probiotics in one drop of breastmilk? If the feds are watching me, I wonder if their goal is to turn me into a giant milk machine. Put me on a pumping machine and make my pump my life away. Living in such a capitalist society, that wouldn't even surprise me. I've always made jokes that I'm like a cow. I can picture them picking me up, strapping me to a machine, and I have to live on a pump – producing milk for a sick world.

Human Experience

The human experience is a trip because of so many layers that exist within us. We have multiple internal emotions and we're constantly navigating the spiritual world and the physical world. The two seem to be connected, however, I think we tend to disconnect them at times. I know I do.

I sound like some hippie-shaman-artist thing. I wish I could just let go of the idea that people are entirely out to get me… but it really does feel that way. Sometimes I catch myself getting so anxious and paranoid. For example, today I was going to take pictures in my journal – but my journal seems to have vanished in the black hole of time. My mind tells me that someone broke into my house and stole the journal for reasons unknown… but my heart doesn't want to believe that's true.

At times, I get so anxious and paranoid, I manifest it all into fruition. I think maybe that's what I did. I still can't say with 100% certainty that's what happened – but I feels like an absolute in my mind and feels intensely real, even when I rationally know it's just my paranoia lying to me.

I constantly swing back and forth on the pendulum of depression to mania. I can't decide which state is more pleasant to live in because they come with their own struggles and their own benefits. The depression side, or as

I like to call it, '"the lesser frequency"' comes with waves of intense lethargy, not getting out of bed, eating more, showering less. It's exhausting. I think mania, or my "elevated state", is more fun to live in – yet when I'm living there, it's exhausting in its own way because it comes with such an intense high. Why is being a human THIS challenging at times? Am I gifted? Or am I just totally crazy? Who knows? It's all up to the perception of the person I'm around.

New Thoughts

New thoughts? Eh, we shall see. I feel like my thoughts just get recycled through every few years. I journal everything and try to keep tabs on my own thoughts… but they still drive in some of the same lanes and head in the same direction. Maybe they change every seven years to be exact considering my first real delusional manic episode was at 19 and then a more severe one happened at 26.

How interesting to think about since our cells are regenerated every seven years.

I'm low-key stressing super hard about finances. I hate the feeling of being behind. Tomorrow I'm going to do some door-dash. Except when tomorrow comes, I won't be able to because things constantly pop up. Oh, life.

Lithium

Every day, I sell my soul to my meds. I wasn't born for this reality, so in order to make the neuro-typicals more comfortable, I swallow the pill and put on the mask… Everyone has one… it's just not fully accepted yet to admit it. People walk around wearing their masks most of the day. They find it hard to take it off out of fear of judgment. Covid made it even easier by providing a physical mask rather than a hypothetical one. I hid behind this for years and when I finally started the process of taking it off, people couldn't handle the energy I had. Even I couldn't handle the energy I had.

Leveling Up

Today I moved up from Level 2 to Level 3, I even was granted privileges, like answering the phone. It's new and exciting. I love the freedom and openness of sound and space. The overstimulation is definitely high because there's a lot of people in comparison that what I was just around. I'm navigating it in a healthy way though and doing my best to keep my head above water.

The level system is weird. I think about it like levels of life. When we're disconnected from people, like in level one, we are stuck in a lower frequency. Being in a lower frequency is nice for my anxious self but it's challenging for this side that wants to connect with others. I feel like I'm suppressed on that level. As if I'm a bad person for wanting to connect. They say it's for my safety… but I struggle to understand why that is. Maybe I'll understand in due time, or maybe I'll never fully grasp it.

Leveling up is beautiful though. I get more privileges, I can meet new people, I can share my story and listen to others share theirs. Leveling up means I'm one step closer to being let out.

Hormones

I'm super biased to think that women's health is a huge contributor to the significance of why we're labeled, "'CRAZY'". Honestly though, birth is an annual traumatic situation. We fluctuate between a euphoric onset of love and serotonin, then, swish! It's vanished like the wind until we catch ourselves grasping onto the life race we call "Existence". It's a whole whirlwind of intense emotion and we're expected to snap right back.

That's not the case though.

Imagine putting your body through intense trauma, draining your hormones into a vortex, and then given a newborn that cries constantly and doesn't sleep. It's the type of challenge none of us can prepare for, including our physical bodies. Women are made to feel guilt or shame if we don't snap right back into society… but HOW are we supposed to after something so crippling?

I struggled with postpartum for months after Marley was born. It took me nearly seven months to start to feel myself again. Then guess what happened; boom – I was pregnant again.

I still haven't recovered from this last birth. Hence the reason I'm writing this from a hospital rather than the comfort of my own home. I like to think I snapped back.

My weight surely did, I ended up even smaller than pre-pregnancy. However, my mind and spiritual self is are still struggling to catch up.

I keep reminding myself that it'll all stabilize soon. I've leveled up and will continue to. I just have to take it a one moment at a time.

Killing Time

How do you kill time during the last few days of psychiatric hold? Read. Lately, I've been reading a lot. Like, a dumb amount honestly. I have my favorites and they help me cope through the unstable moments. Today it's "'It's Kind of a Funny Story'" and also "'The Story of Pat'.' If you're anything like me though, meaning you're high energy, reading doesn't quite cut it. I've been waking up in the middle of the night just to write or draw. That's what slows the thoughts down. Oh and meds, had to cave and take an Ativan because I'm too awake for life right now.

Oh, life. What is it and why is it happening?

I can feel today is going to be a good day. I'm thinking of Eric and hoping he's doing well. Whenever certain people pop up in my dreams, I always want to check in to see how they're doing. I love seeing him happy and thriving in Portland, however, I wish he was closer. Maybe it's best for the both of us that he branched out. I want him to be in the safe space to be doing well and I also want to allow the same for myself.

Ugh, I miss Bailey too. I've thought about him a ton and can't wait to hear his voice. He's such a great human. I can't believe I was so delusional, I thought he was taking us off in the Musk spaceship to be probed by aliens. Yep, that's right… I 100% thought that. Literally WHAT. The mind is such a wild space to exist sometimes.

My delusions come and go like little pictures in my head. I'm stable and '"on the right track working my ass off to stay".' So far, I'm doing great, despite here and there paranoia. The nurses have really helped with that so far. I'm going to send them a thank you card when I leave for sure.

I can't wait to hear my kid's voices when my dad calls back. They're such a grounding vessel of human for me. There isn't a word in the world that encompasses how much I love my babies. They truly are my entire universe.

Ulterior Motives

I can't stand feeling like people have ulterior motives. It's much worse in the morning than in the day… Maybe my energy is too loud sometimes. Or maybe I exist on a different frequency. Who knows? Even though it can be true that people have ulterior motives, it shouldn't hold me off from the potential of seeing good things in others and not focusing on the negative loop. I just need to stay true to who I am.

Gah, I just hope I'm getting there.

I'm not the only one who struggles with delusional thinking. I try to remind myself of this constantly. Whenever Angelo is getting ready to leave the house, he cycles through negative thoughts. For example, our BLM flag has been hanging up for a while and he's always paranoid someone is going to kill us over it. He seems to forget that we're surrounded by a strong community of good people though.

Sometimes I have to set my anxieties aside and be present in hopes that he'll learn how to navigate his own anxieties without me helping him through it.

Or maybe we'll just struggle for eternity. Again… what is life?

Boundaries

The pandemic has drastically changed the world. I feel like our immune systems are at such a loss and the only way to get back out there is to do so in a new light; safety, love, empathy, and compassion.

I still enjoy wearing a mask in some situations. I prefer to read the room and see where others are at and make a decision. We have to wear it all the time here in the hospital and that definitely gets annoying. But honestly, it IS a hospital and I need to just adjust and get used to it.

I woke up from a nap meditation. First time I've napped in a while. The meds must be working a bit – yay. I have visions of what my reality will look like when I get out of here and it seems promising. I picture myself maskless, physically and spiritually. I also want to be aware of my energy and those around me. I've made a list of reasonable boundaries. They go as followed;

- *ask questions*
- *be there (mentally, emotionally, and physically)*
- *don't be too vulnerable right away*
- *set up for success*
- *have quality times over quantity*
- *avoid enmeshment*

_ *don't be afraid to fail*

_ *don't gaslight, stone-wall, over exert, or give too much*

_ *Remember: you can't pour from an empty cup.*

Boundaries

Oh wow, what a beautiful life with intricate sadness at times. I feel I have two souls within me – one that slings down to the depths of nothingness and one that slowly rises to the level of the Gods'. A light that shines, at times, too bright and then at other times, dims and burns out. The beauty of a walking trauma response bundled up with unique flowers that both bloom and wither.

I don't know what's going on… but I know it's a lot.

I continually ask myself questions throughout the day, such; "'who are you?" "If not now, then when?" "What part of your needs healing?" "WHY.'".

I wish I knew all of the answers, but the questions are asked in a way that seems senseless to make certain of. Nothing makes my brain spin out more than the desire to seek out everything.

The Moment

Saturday's are for re-charging. The rain is pouring, haven't been outside for group all day. Dying for some fresh air but embracing the moment with coloring and writing.

My brain is slowing down, but my body is still all over the place. Overall, I'm way more clear headed than I was just a few weeks ago. It's amazing what can go on when you have the right medicine combination. I like to think of my brain as an egg… scrambled, boiled, or soft. Currently, it feels soft.

I'm aching to hold my babies and cuddle Angelo. Soon enough. As I would say to Marley, "Two more sleeps." I got this. I've been really starting to process my psychosis episode and coming to terms with the lost grip on reality that I had.

Things I believed in my manic episode:

- *Aliens were abducting us*
- *Russia had taken over*
- *We're in a simulation*
- *Feds were stealing my answers*
- *The male species was dying off*
- *I was part of a big series/game show*

- *Angelo and I were going to save our species by procreating*
- *Robots had entirely taken over*

Things that helped pull me out of mania:

- *Medication*
- *Showering*
- *Grounding techniques*
- *Eating/drinking healthy*
- *being around support*
- *Art/writing*
- *Music*
- *Gratitude lists*
- *Reading*
- *Communicating*

I've also been consistently reminding myself that some of the greatest people alive deal with mental illness. If they can achieve greatness with a disability, – so can I.

God?

I get out in two days and all I can think about is playing with the kids, cuddling Angelo, and being present with my sweet family.

Going into a full psychosis is one of the most intense, spiritually energized experiences I've ever had. I can no longer define myself as an atheist. It broke a ton of borders and boxes I've subscribed to and showed me how much is truly unknown about the human body.

I think a lot of artists grasp this and it makes sense why it could push us to insanity…

The Universe is complex and ever evolving. I want and desire to see every inch of it. Every multiverse within the universe. The expanding nothingness and everything-ness of human existence.

Residual Side Effects

I have a strong feeling they may up my meds today, but that's okay. I'm still very hypomanic. No major delusions, just a little paranoia. Lucky for me, I remember my coping skills and I'm able to navigate it much better these days.

I've been listening to a ton of the Shaky Hands. It's funny how many cycles I've gone through with them. I'm so happy to be feeling good and stable. I hope the doctor's recognize all of the hard work I've put in.

Today's goals:

- *stay stable*
- *Communicate*
- *Work with the nurses on discharge*
- *Call Angelo, dad*
- *Be nice to myself*
- *Do yoga*
- *Write in my journal*
- *Eat healthy*
- *Breathe.*

Random… but what do you think is worse, an ornery old person or a creepy, old person?

I would have to go with the creepy, old person.

Fly Away

Life could be gone in seconds and the reality is that we're just a small glimpse of it. I think the most important thing we can all do is be kind and love another. It's all anyone can ask for honestly.

Angelo was so funny I called the other day. I said, "My burger is amazing!" In my delusional state, I thought he was a professional cook for the hospital and had made the burger especially for me. He immediately informed me that he didn't, in fact, make the burger but he was happy I loved it. For what it's worth, he must realize how much I love him considering he and the babies are my sole focus no matter what dimension or reality I'm living in.

This morning/night shift nurse is making it near impossible to pump and it's driving me mad. I get that she's tired or maybe confused but navigating breastfeeding in the hospital has been way more difficult than I think it should be. It feels like I'm just hand expressing engorged tits at all times. GAH – drying up a supply I brutal. Especially when I have made an oversupply.

Oh well, I shall survive. Taking it a moment at a time and going to read my book until people or the dayshift comes to help to switch things up a bit.

I'm A Cow

I just got out of the shower, and I still feel so engorged. It's insane because I haven't breastfed milo Milo in two weeks, yet I'm still spilling milk out of my boobs like a damn cow. On top of it, I can feel myself getting slightly delusional again. I'm trying to breathe through it and remember that I'm not alone in my thoughts. Many other people feel the same way and struggle with the same thoughts.

My medicine makes made such a huge difference so far. I'm excited to get out and feel back to normal – if that ever happens. I'm especially excited to see my sweet babies. If I get mixed up again, someone just turn me around and I promise I'll make it through.

I'm at the beginning of the maze, but I know I'll make it to the end through handwork and resilience. There're many things I can rely on to make it through each moment. I just need to hold my lips and own my shit… and if that doesn't work, be like the birds in the sky and fly free.

If people were to count how many times a day they struggle with intrusive thoughts, like physically count, I bet we would learn more about numbers and the patterns within in them rather than the intrusive thoughts that distract us away from the bigger picture.

Processing

Is this where it begins? The tears flow out and the processing starts to take place? The superwoman hides away while the dark clouds loom overhead.

The flood gates have officially opened big time and I'm scared. I'm scared I'm never going to see my kids again or that there's something diabolically wrong with me. I want to crawl into a small pod with Angelo and the babies and feel the warmth surrounding us. I want to feel okay, again. I NEED to feel okay again.

I despise when I can physically feel the shift in my mood. I can go from the brightest shining star to a swirling black hole within seconds.

How is it sustainable to live this way? I can read everything when looking into someone's eyes, yet I feel like no one can read mine. I like to believe the pandemic helped this for people, helped make it easier to read other's eyes when half of their face is covered. I think we still struggle with that disconnect though. I feel so disconnected.

I think there's a super power that comes from reading eyes. Being able to read the emotion and unsaid thoughts of a person. Only certain people can and Covid made it even stronger.

I hope someone reads my eyes soon and saves me from myself. Sometimes I'm my own worst enemy. My mind can be such a looming place of intense scrutiny.

To move forward, I need to just lean into the storm.

Tacos

He started talking about what kind of tacos he would eat if he could and, for some reason, I loved it. Tacos are always forever a love language to me. The different styles, the flavor, the mixed, and the amazing different ways you can make them.

If my life were a movie, tacos would be the main course meal. Made with love by Angelo.

Letter

Dear Ciara,

Learning that you do indeed have bipolar is quite the conundrum. You denied it for such a long time and disguised it so well. How were you honestly supposed to know of the little beast that lied within you? You masked up well! Championship well. I'm proud of you for being strong. You continue to power on despite any hardships you may face. It's amazing, honestly. Your mind is a place of exuberant adventure, and it only makes sense to feel trapped inside at times.

Remember to breathe and take control of what is in your control – YOU. Even when it feels otherwise. You're in control of how you respond to each situation and you're doing great.

Mixed State

My "'roomie'" is out. It's adorable. I've been sleeping hard but feeling too excited to see Angelo and the babies it's made it hard to get adequate rest because of this. Coming down from a manic episode means a lot to process, I think. I'm trying not to let it overwhelm me, but mania is wild.

My light can shine as bright as I choose for it to, or it can dim to a flickering flame. I have to speak with my heart to accomplish anything.

Existing in a mixed state, being both manic and intensely depressed, is like trying to peel back layers of my skin but not knowing what's underneath. It's like one minute I feel totally charged and the next I feel completely empty.

Being in this state makes me slightly concerned for my release only because I'm afraid they won't deem me fit. My game plan for release is:

- *call counselor*
- *Explain and be open*
- *Family support*
- *Pay attention to warning signs and listen to them*
- *Allow room for growth*
- *Be patient with self*

- *Focus on family and school*
- *Don't burnout*

There are multiple things I'm looking forward to upon release, but it's primarily; Angelo, the babies, and simple luxuries (like a bath).

Not getting enough sleep seems to be one of the biggest contributors to my mania so I've been doing my best to relax enough to get rest. I seem to be waking up way too early and I'm trying to get it in check.

Some other things that trigger me are;

- *loud sounds*
- *Certain tones*
- *Changes in routine*
- *Large groups*
- *Death*

With that being said, there's a million and one ways I can practice calming myself down, for example; tea, medicine, walks, writing, reading, meditation, family, and art. I need to consistently remind myself that I am good enough. I am not my thoughts. I can do great things.

I feel like something bad is looming over me. I got this though. I am in control of how I respond to my surroundings. I need to disconnect and reconnect at the same down.

Disassociated

I'm constantly fluctuating between a sense of hyperawareness and a sense of disassociation. I know it'll be okay because sometimes it makes the music sound better and the food taste better… yet I know that soon will come the crashing helplessness of uncertainty. It's wild having two polarizing characters when all I wanna do is have them under control and feel I know how I'm going to feel from one minute to the next. My roommate is quietly sleeping while I've been awake since 2:30.

I'm happy but I'm sad. How am I supposed to feel comfortable in this body when my mind can't makeup what's happening? I feel as though I am walking on eggshells while simultaneously walking through the clouds of heaven. My brain just wants to explode.

Travel

I wonder what it's like to travel through South America. I've always had a strong pull towards Brazil... I have no idea why other than the desire to be immersed in another culture. I want to learn everything I can about every culture and be able to share what makes up ours. I'm fascinated by intercultural connections. I'm wanderlust and as wandering and waving as the ocean that surrounded our border. I want to know each and everything I can know before I make the departure from this Earth.

I remind myself constantly of the most important things in life. I think of myself as a small speck of dust in an expanding Universe of time and space. If I was to ever immerse myself in another culture, I would need to do so in the most kind and loving way. I never want to represent our culture, the American culture, in a negative light. I feel America struggles with this currently... but it's up to the individuals to change that narrative.

Pulsing

I'm so confused by the court system. They're saying I'm on a hold but there was a chance I was being released today and now I'm not… so why is that exactly?

My pulse is really high. It feels like everyone is kinda upset towards me. Maybe it's in my mind or maybe I'm tapping into an intuition I didn't know I had until today.

The man in the mirror is the one who has a strong opinion of one's own self. Be grateful in order to fill my sole purpose in life. We have to keep moving forward and try our best to deliver one another to the next step.

This lovely little lady once told me that she thought I was beautiful, I agreed and carried on. Sometimes it's as simple as that, sometimes it's as complex as overthinking a compliment and turning it into something it wasn't intended to be.

My mother once said she would fight for me, and I knew she would. I know she is. I want to be released from this prison, not only in my mind, but the physical hold of being at the hospital. I'm ready to depart.

Free From Concern

Today is so hard. I thought I was doing okay but I'm dizzy and very lightheaded, totally out of it. I'm ready to go home.

Forgive me for all the sins of my past and please let me move toward the light. I want to be cleansed of my wrong-doings and be reminded of my rights. My accomplishments are; my babies, my relationship, my fight, my love.

I am a fighter through and through. I get triggered into fight and flight mode because of the generational traumas of my past and other's past. I feel it so deeply.

We all cope differently but I think the basis of what we all desire is to feel connected. I acted erratically because my fight or flight was pushed to the max. '"Jacob's Ladder".' I feel trapped in Hell when I'm this disconnected. The in-between is the middle/main and until I'm reunited with my babies and husband, I don't think I'll feel like I'm in heaven. Maybe I'm an angel, fallen and confused. Maybe I'm a human stuck in the middle. Or maybe I just don't know.

I wanted to believe there's good in everyone, but I know that's not the case. I've seen the evil, I've felt it. At times, I think I've even acted on it in small ways.

I forgive myself and the rest of my family for the sins of their past. I don't know the details, but I know they feel terrible for certain actions. I want them to be free of this concern. I see them in my dreams, and I want them to feel free from heartache.

Intuition

What if this book is all that's left of me when I make the great departure? Sometimes I think, actually ALWAYS, I think of scenarios in which I am the fallen angel and I have to find my way back. How am I supposed to do that without help though? I need help.

I know my mom's helping. I can feel the presence of my dad. I can see and smell Deena in the nurses… but I have failed by not moving forward.

Treat everyone with eternal kindness. That's all I feel I can offer, yet the people pushing me back think differently. I feel as if they want me to fail or something. I get confused every moment about what I'm supposed to do. Maybe that's just it – maybe I'm not supposed to do anything. Or maybe it's all of it. There's a God, but we have to actively stay sane while riding the waves.

I'm currently stuck in my past self, but I know with work and rest, I'll make it to my present. The present is challenging to practice when you're mentally ill though. I keep hoping for a miracle without realizing I'm already in one.

The biggest battle is being away from my kids. I wish I could kiss and squeeze them. I miss them SO much. I just want to hold them and look into their eyes again. Oh, my heart.

If you were going through the depths of Hell, would you try your best to make it out or would you give up?

The Giving Tree

Every time I talk to Angelo, I feel more in tune. What a weird love language of beauty and all synchronicities. I'm so grateful for him.

I love giving; it's all I can do with absolute care and genuine compassion. I want to leave a positive impact on each person I meet and be able to identify my struggles before they turn into larger struggles. PTSD is a trip. Yesterday the charge nurse decided I was going back to the isolation room, and it sent me into a full fight or flight response. I can't handle the idea of being completely isolated. It makes me want to lose my mind. Lack of control is not my friend.

The hospital is confusing and not helping with my mania at all. I asked for headphones and actually just got done doing a meditation with it that was really relaxing. It's hard to sleep when I'm not home though – which in turn drives my mania back up. It's a weird up and down fluctuation… but I'm getting there.

My court hearing is in the morning tomorrow and then they determined my next step. Either I have to go to the hospital for two months or I get to go home. I'm ready to talk to the DE and hopefully move forward from this mess.

Life has felt way too intense lately and I just don't know how to navigate such big emotions. I'm hoping that the lithium starts to kick in and really help settle my nerves. It's impossible for me to sleep here and it makes my situation worse. I'm just attempting to take it one day at a time.

I just wish I could go with the flow like the fish do.

Pre-Court

Court tomorrow and they just upped my meds again. Looks like I'm on lithium, zyprexa, and Ativan. Ugh, the "patient" game is really challenging. I'm doing well today, no delusions. Last night, I was having them and they were pretty severe. I thought we were all stuck in the in-between.

Wouldn't that be wild, though? I felt like I was on Jacob's ladder because the nurse's name was Jacob. I felt bad because it took six security guards to finally sedate me. I feel like I'm a scrappy little thing. One of the guards was getting a little too into his role and looked excited about it all for some reason. Ugh, what a trip.

Being bipolar is weird but being schizoaffective is a whole other kind of trip. I hate how the delusions can be so real and intense. Like I 100% believed my soul was being torn out of me yesterday.

I also think Covid really changed shit because people don't know how to interact anymore, and everything is based on eye emotion and lack of transparency. The pandemic changed a lot for a ton of humans and I'm' not surprised at all to see it… Just slightly sad.

Hearing Marley and Milo's voice yesterday was amazing. I'm proud of how big they're getting and how fast they're developing. They have such an indescribable bond.

I'm stoked that Angelo and I decided to take the leap and have two instead of just Marley. They really make life feel much better and brighter.

Angelo's Letter

My dearest Ciara,

I love you so, so much. Our kids love you so much. You are such an amazing mom. I'm so happy that we have each other in this beautiful universe. You are an amazingly strong, smart, beautiful, and kind being. This world would feel very empty without you. I'm always here for you and I will never stop loving you. You're my best friend. Let's keep building this wonderful life we have. I love you so much.

Breastfeeding

I didn't realize my last time breastfeeding Milo would be quite literally my last time. It pulls at my heart strings in a number of ways. I just want to hold him and cuddle him. I want to nurse him and be there for him and Marley when they cry. I feel so helpless here. They are the most perfect little beans I could ever hope for.

The last time I nursed Milo, I remember I was slightly frustrated. He kept pinching me and holding down on me. I felt like I needed him to stop… but didn't know what to do. Unfortunately, I was forced into a much needed vacation and now I don't have a choice about stopping.

Breastfeeding is truly amazing. There are over one billion probiotics in one single drop of breastmilk. Imagine if we used it like a medicine. I guarantee we could cure some illnesses that way.

Passed Over

I love seeing the past over in my dreams. Last night, I had a dream I saw Hunter and got to talk to him. It was random, but super cool. I like to daydream about what my friends that have passed would be doing right now. Would we be on similar paths? Vastly different?

Passing over is the real journey. I think we tend to get stuck on the present or the past and forget about the beauty of the future. So many people are afraid of death… but for some reason, it's never scared me a ton. I like to imagine that we have multiple lives that we never truly die, we're just reborn again.

I also like to think that's what dreams are for. I see dead people in my dreams all the time. I imagine that's how they communicate with me. In my dreams, I'm always running. Just like Forest Gump, running wild and free. Maybe I should take up jogging when I get out. It's a healthy outlet and it feels pretty good.

I often ponder how other people think things through. I have songs playing in my head while also having multiple voices talking to one another while also seeing pictures.

I think it's primarily like that because I'm still hypomanic. I can recognize now what helps me avoid mania… but I still struggle to get the racing thoughts under control once they begin.

Maybe I'm still stuck in the in-between. Or maybe I'm just not designed for this reality.

Court Hearing

Today is my court hearing. I'm feeling jittery and nervous, but I'm excited to take a step in a new direction. I just finished my morning calls; Angelo, Dad, and Mom. Dad is taking the kids to daycare this morning which I imagine to be so cute. He asked me how to do Marley's hair… gosh I miss her a ton.

It's a long windy road, the one I'm on, but I know we'll get there soon. Hoping with all that's in me that court goes well.

I feel so exhausted at times and burnt out, like the same day is replaying but with different options. I just want to go to sleep and wake up refreshed… but that isn't an option in the hospital because I can't relax. It's not necessarily an option out of here either because the babies pull me in different directions constantly as well.

I would rather have the kids pull me than navigate being away from them though. They will always be my number one. Can't imagine life any other way.

Freedom

Tell the world... I'm leaving today! I'm so happy. I'm going to pick up the kids and they have no idea I'm coming. It's going to be a much needed surprise. I can't wait to see Marlcy's sweet face and bubba's big boy smile.

Things to remember during discharge;

- *take meds*
- *Meditate*
- *Exercise*
- *Communicate*
- *Follow-up*
- *Keep journaling*

It feels surreal that I finally get to leave. I started crying when the judge said I could. It's been an intense couple of weeks, a literal war in my mind. I'm grateful to be climbing out on the other side.

Proud of myself. I got this.

Home

62

Being back home is wildly weird. I'm much happier to be in the comfort of my home, but its 4:30 and I'm already up for the day. I think I might go jogging to burn some energy. It's challenging. To know what to do. I have an irrational fear that if I go jogging, I'll be arrested or something. For what? I have no idea. My brain is just a dark place at times.

I think our dreams predict our future sometimes if we know how to tap into it correctly. I've had many dreams where I'm like, "I could see that happening.". Then it either happens or something similar happens. I've heard it called Deja vu before.

Sometimes I'll have a dream inside of a dream. Those are always the drippiest because I can't distinguish reality from the subconscious for a second. This morning I had a dream that I was rocking with Milo, which I was actually doing for a second late at night, but then I had a dream. So when I woke up from the dream, my physical self was very confused for a second.

Have you ever had a dream inside of a dream that made you slightly lose your grip on reality?

Family

Marley's energy is loud, just like mine. Being in the room with three generations all together is beyond intense.

It's been a great day so far, despite the loud energy. My mania is still lingering around. Angelo and I walked around stores and thirsted. I kept imagining that we were walking in the Metaverse. Sometimes I get lost in derealization and feel like we are. I followed the signs and got things that felt right in the moment.

I love Angelo so much it hurts. Life is beautiful together and I can't imagine anyone else I would want by my side. When he and I are in sync, we flow together like the fish in the sea… towards the good and away from the bad. We plant the seeds of our future.

Today genuinely has been such a great day. The weather is perfect, we thrifted, and then we came home and all made dinner together. I don't know where I'd be in life without them, but I know I'm so grateful to have them by my side.

Our community is wonderful.

I had a dream last night that Angelo and I were racing through time, tornado, and hurricanes to get to the babies. Once we got to them, they were fine. It solidified how safe I feel with their teachers. It's nice to know they're in a safe space when I leave them at daycare because being back in school and at home is very intense. One day at a time is all I can do – which is enough right now.

Digital Age

The digital age is wild. By wild, I mean, completely unsustainable. I feel like we're headed towards another industrial revolution and the working class is being gentrified out to the suburbs.

The technological boom we've experienced is detrimental to our planet and I don't think any of us know how to reverse the damage that's been done. We can continue to invent things and attempt solutions, but overall, we've reached an unsustainable way of living with tech.

I've been up since 3:30 am. My internal clock is all screwed up. I'm up at 3:30, asleep by 9. At least I'm getting some rest. I just hate waking up before the sun. It makes me feel guilty. Sometimes it feels like we're all just born into the same day, just different outcomes and solutions.

Life is one massive trip.

Poem

My baby, my world. She's truly my everything. As is he.

They make me feel like every day, everything, is going to be alright.

Even with the high-pitched screams and constant clutter, I am filled with joy just to know they're here.

The way they look into my soul... A world still unknown.

Dream On

You want to learn the facts? The truth? Me fuckin' too. What if it's all just a dream and our dreams are reality? Every time you close your eyes, you are faced with choices. Then when you open your eyes, it's a chance to reset.

Coming out of a manic high feels coming down from a ton of drugs and desperately hoping that some of you stays sane to be insane at times. Insane people are the ones who get shit done on this plant. It's where comedians thrive.

Pieces of me feel like there's a ton of humans connected to the ventilators at the hospital and the alt-right is slowly taking over by hospitalizing the lefties (or the weaklings). Oh many... what a trip to think about. I hope I'm so wrong.

I wish I knew how to test this theory out though. Without being disruptive that is. Honestly, what better way to control a group of people than to hook them up to ventilators until they crack.

However! I don't think anyone is necessarily in on it. Just random brain waves. I'm grateful to be out. The hospital gives me a ton of anxiety. It's ironic since me Wanted to work in one. Maybe I should just work at a private clinic or remote. I will find out in due time.

Innocence

I've got a war in my mind and it's eating me alive. I miss the innocence of childhood. Sometimes it feels like I'm genuinely suffocating as an adult. I can remember feeling like the entire world was my oyster… but not so much anymore.

Stay true to who you are but constantly improve into who you aspire to be. That's the way I keep going on the hard days. Especially the days I feel trapped and misunderstood.

Simple days seem to slow me down while simultaneously hyping me up. I feel as if I've existed in a mixed state for roughly a week. It's like I'm walking on egg-shells in my own body. Ultimately, I'm on the up and up. I've been around my family 24/7. I'm feeling less anxious each day.

Maybe.

The Coast

I definitely still feel like I'm being watched to some degree. However, I don't feel it's negative if so. I'm trying to keep a positive mindset.

I want out of Coeur d'Alene soon. I want a big house on the coast and minimal worries. I want to walk on the beach each day and wake up with the goal of doing work remotely.

Ah, who knows what the future holds.

The little things can be the biggest triggers. Marley being put in timeout and screaming for her baby while Angelo said no to her is one of my biggest trigger buttons. I can feel it in my whole entire body. The push/pull of fighting for my life while I'm being forced to be separated from my kids.

Triggers are seriously the worst though. Sometimes, almost every night actually, I'll wake up sweating profusely and freaking out. PTSD is wild. I can't imagine trying to navigate this without my meds. I'm happy I've come in just a couple of weeks... but I'm also excited to feel less paranoid.

Mood Ring

According to my mood ring, I'm happy. Which I agree with. Despite still being manic, I'm feeling okay (I think). Do we ever fully know…? I'd like to think so, but who actually knows. I feel loved, which is amazing. I can tell Angelo loves me more than life and that makes my heart beam because SAME. Also, same with the babies.

Keeping myself rooted in reality has been one of the biggest struggles in the last month. I keep trailing off into the land of disassociation. It's where I find myself living ever so often. All that exists though is the present moment and our connection to it.

My present moment;

- *Notebook*
- *Water running*
- *Sound machine*
- *Heavy eyes*
- *Itchy throat*
- *Music in the background*

Another crazy thought I've had today is, *"what if the only war that exists is the war we're constantly navigating In our own minds?"* The other physical wars are manifested evils of war criminals who carry out the atrocities of man. What would you do if you knew you were at war? I personally would treat all with love and kindness. It's all I ever want to do to be honest. It's all I know how to do. Even when the guards tried to break me into the hospital, I put their needs above mine. I was parched and in need of water after having my back stepped on for minutes. When they grabbed me water, my first reaction was to give it to the guard that nearly killed me. His mouth was dry, and he was out of breath. I knew the fight he was going through because I went through it with him. I knew he needed water because I needed water.

I don't know how to be any other way than empathetic. It's both a gift and a curse.

Hello World

I've been waking up early and having the mornings to myself which is pretty nice. I feel like an exhausted machine. Like a robot that's only half way charged but never completely dies. My battery is running low but I'm still going. It's tiring sometimes.

I woke up from a dream about grandma. She was in the hospital; I was a nurse (I think) and we were pacing around worrying about her. I genuinely think dreams have a bit too much truth to them sometimes. We just need to know how to tap into it. Our dreams can literally manifest the physical world if we believe in it enough.

"Think big thoughts, but relish small pleasures."

When I fall asleep lately, I go into the deepest sleep immediately. It feels like time traveling, but I wake up and I'm still in this plane of existence.

Paranoia has been a really challenging emotion to navigate. I fluctuate between highs and lows. The lows come with unsettling paranoia and the highs come with race thoughts. Put that all together and it makes for quite an interesting existence.

"Leave everything a little better than you found it."

What Will I Do

What in the world am I going to do with this book when I'm done with it? Am I ever really done with it though? I like to think that millions of people will read it and love it, but who knows. That would require work and I don't even know how to take the first step.

Maybe it'll publish itself. Wouldn't that be great? I'm hungry, that's all.

Prisoner

I think I'm a prisoner of war, but the war is either in my mind for in another dimension of the multiverse. I can feel it, hear it, and smell it at times. It's an absolute. Yet most people can't even comprehend what I'm saying when I try to talk about it. I wish I knew someone who understood the intricacies of my thoughts.

We are all time travelers in the warp of spatial vastness.

I also think we're created simply to create Products for production. Engineers of time. Blimps in the machine. We can do anything we put our mind to… but first we must learn the mind. We are solely responsible for what we give our energy to.

I AM enough.

Patterns

I see patterns everywhere. In the grocery store, out eating, in the house. While, yes, it's a manifestation of my illness, it's also something that's unexplainable in my opinion.

I talk about something, visualize it, then it happens. I'd be so grateful to be experiencing IT. Whatever IT is.

The patterns I see are pretty amazing manifestations of my mind… but sometimes they can be slightly scary. Like when the sounds amplify or when the physical sensations take over.

Maybe it's mania. Or maybe it's because I'm a Sagittarius or maybe it's because I'm secretly gifted. No matter what the reason, it's wild to feel it in its entirety. I'm grateful for a grain that fires neurons quickly. I just have to learn how to channel it all in a healthy way.

Detached

Our world is slowly dying, and I feel helpless to its needs. We have the biggest carbon impact. I hold onto and remind myself of the things that motivate me to do well... my babies, good music, Angelo, powerful people like Malcom X and Gandhi, writing, drawing, connecting, and school.

I need to learn to detach from the lies my ADHD and Bipolar tell me. The "'you care too much'" or "'be better, you suck".' They're just cruel and based on lies. I want to be able to separate them from myself and remember who I TRULY am. Not what my brain decides to think I am at certain moments.

The reality is that we're all emotional beings. We get lost in the weeds when our world is actually our oyster. We all deserve love and respect; we all should give love and respect. In order to progress, we must take the initial step. We deserve to be our own heroes. We deserve basic respect.

I AM enough.

I never cared for about guns. Which is funny as an "Idaho girl". With that being said, I do want to learn more about self-defense and know what to do in an escalated situation.

Going to school for chemistry and forensics is a big step towards understanding the human experience. I want to know how to protect myself and my family in situations that put me at risk. I want more street smarts to ease my paranoia. Although I know my delusions are false, sometimes they feel very real.

I like to envision my thoughts as a package on a conveyer belt or a river with leaves floating down. My thoughts are the item… they float or drift by and then they're followed by another. It's important to maintain mental focus and remember that I am worthy of good things.

One day, the prisoner will be set free. It's up to me to work towards that though.

Consciousness

What if death is just a social construct created by man and we have infinite lives? I think about this a lot. Sometimes I even pretend I'm already dead. I imagine I'm walking amongst fallen angels and we're all just in a special later of the in-between. A special layer of consciousness.

Oh, what a time. It makes my mind spin and somewhat race when I get stuck in this thinking pattern. I imagine I'm never going to get out. In my eyes though, I'm in heaven when I'm with the babies and Angelo. As long as we're united and I know they're safe. Hell is nonexistent to me.

It was only during my separation from them that I felt Hell was amongst me. It was only during the disconnect from humans that I felt I had been dragged there.

We think we control ourselves, that we have control. Our brains control us though, we don't have control when the brain takes over. We have to try and find beauty in the loss of control though. We have the power to have a good attitude and treat others with respect.

In order to rise about the breakdown, we must act with love, and we must encompass the light we all hold within us.

There's beauty in the breakdown sometimes. I truly believe it's in the depths of our worst moments, the moments that make us feel we're never be able to make it, that we grow the most. Some call it trauma, some call it art. No matter what you call it… it gives us spirit.

My spirit can't die.

My Spirit

My spirit lives high in the clouds of uncertainty. One with edge of "'what if'" and "'why not'?' It makes sense even though I endlessly struggle to make sense of it.

I've been out of the hospital for two weeks now and life is slowly beginning to feel more stable. I think I'm still very delusional though and I can't distinguish reality from my own mind at times. I sometimes wish I still had more focused energy. My energy levels are still high, but it's hard to concentrate on the task at hand.

The kids are extremely over stimulating. Bubba is currently being a tornado and Marley just talks endlessly. Being a mom to kids eighteen months apart is the hardest job I've ever done. I don't know how full-time stay at home moms do it all the time. I feel exhausted.

Takeover

I think if a country was going to take-over, they would do it through technology, not necessarily bomb. Tech is the cornerstone of America, and we don't function well without it. We would be lost if it was all hacked.

It's terrifying to think of a world without tech. everything we do is rooted in it. Like right now, I'm listening *"Phoenix"* on my phone. Music always eases my anxiety. It's essential.

Tech is intense. Amazing, yet intense. Everything in this state of consciousness is fluid. No moment in time is fixed. All we can do is be kind to one another and walk in our own lane. The lane of uncertainty mixed with emotional damage.

All we know and all we are is figments of the mind's imagination. We can accomplish anything we want. The human brain is much more complex than anything we can put into words. Some of the greatest people "'lost'" their minds. In my opinion though, they just learned how to navigate it differently.

The observable Universe; starts, planets, and the sky… wouldn't exist to an individual if that individual ceased to exist. Meaning: our observations are merely the center of our universe. A universe that's multi-layered, like the consciousness we hold within us.

No experience is unique, yet no experience is exactly the same. We, ourselves, are the observable Universe and we hold all the answers we seek to find.

Albert Einstein tested this with the theory of relativity. You know what's crazy about his story? So many people thought he was insane. He didn't even finish high school… yet he's known as one of the most brilliant minds to date.

Don't let others dictate your fate.

Time TRAVEL

Maybe we're just little brain cells stuck inside of an alien brain. Ugh… my brain hurts.

With that being said though, time travel is entirely possible, I think. We have to know how to tap into that layer of consciousness, but I think humans know how to travel time. If we are the creators of the Universe and we know how to tap into stuff like time travel – we also have to know how to tap out of it and be present. I think that's what we all ultimately crave.

I know I crave presence. Living in the past is challenging. Sitting with the heart-ache, my illness has caused the people I love around me to be extremely challenging because I can't stop thinking of what I put them through. I feel immense guilt and sorrow for how my episode caused so many layers of trauma.

How privileged am I though? To have people that love me unconditionally that it killed them to see me struggle. I feel eternally grateful. It's a heavy weight to carry. Love, that is. They all wanted to help me; they still do. But there's nothing anyone could've done. It worked out exactly as it was supposed to. I truly was in another realm of reality, another world. It was like an episode of Black Mirror, and I was the star… except I didn't accept the role yet.

I strive to grow from this destruction. I will plant the seeds of love and worthiness and I will rise to my highest bloom.

Seeds

I want to immerse myself in another culture one day. I think the idea of learning about the diversity of another culture could be extremely rewarding and vital to my growth as a human. It would shape my perspective in many ways.

I am constantly reminding myself of the importance of staying cautious about the thoughts I plant in my mind. Those thoughts will eventually look and grow into fruition. If we think good things, good things will happen, if we think bad things, we will see negative results.

Our life is our thoughts. Plant seeds that flourish and bloom. If your thoughts were rooted in reality, what would you picture?

I'm feeling racy and thinking of a million things to do. So many ideas, so little time. I try to remember, "One moment at a time and I can accomplish many things."

We all have a purpose.

I keep feeling anxious that my manic episode is going to swing to a depressive episode. I shared about my struggles with that thought pattern, as well as my struggles with body dysmorphia, today in group. Everyone was kind

AND UPLIFTING. IT'S NICE TO BE AROUND OTHERS WHO EXPERIENCE SIMILAR BATTLES WITH THEMSELVES.

This Is It

So this is it. My final couple pages of the journal to my madness. There's are many things I want to take away and remember from this journal… first being my growth. I want to keep going, be still with my heart, and cherish small acts of kindness. I'm grateful for my babies, my husband, group, art, writing, and the weather. My goals are to keep progressing forward, start a new journal, and stay grounded. I can achieve all of these goals by communicating, staying healthy, and practicing self-care.

I must always remember that I have the ability to make any day amazing. As do you. We are all just mirrored reflections of one another. While some of us may have mental illness, others maybe the anchors keeping us grounded. I may not exist in this reality… but I have the power to make this reality worth existing in.

Keep going, love. You are much more than you give yourself credit for.